Entrepreneur
kids

All About Social Media

By the Staff of Entrepreneur Media

Entrepreneur
PRESS.

T0125834

Entrepreneur Press, Publisher
Consulting Editor: Michelle Martinez
Cover Design: Andrew Welyczko
Production and Composition: AbandonedWest Creative, Inc.

An application to register this book for cataloging has been submitted to the Library of Congress.

ISBN 978-1-64201-142-5 (paperback) | ISBN 978-1-61308-455-7 (ebook)

Printed in the United States of America

25 24 23 22 21 10 9 8 7 6 5 4 3 2 1

References

Bova, Dan. "How This 18-Year-Old High School Student Built a 6-Figure Social Media Consulting Business." *Entrepreneur Magazine*, Irvine, CA. https://www.entrepreneur.com/article/362401

Eadicicco, Lisa. "How to Create Super-Strong Passwords to Protect Yourself from the 'Heartbleed' Security Bug." *Entrepreneur Magazine*, Irvine, CA. https://www.entrepreneur.com/article/232957

Herzog, Kenny. "At Age 12, He Was Cyberbullied on YouTube. By 15, He Was Running a Profitable Marketing Agency for Instagram Stars." *Entrepreneur Magazine*, Irvine, CA. https://www.entrepreneur.com/article/366185

Newlands, Murray. "Low Productivity? You May Need a Digital Detox." *Entrepreneur Magazine*, Irvine, CA. https://www.entrepreneur.com/article/282940

Prajapati, Chirag. "Here's How Privacy is Threatened by AR/VR." *Entrepreneur Magazine*, Irvine, CA. https://www.entrepreneur.com/article/312280

Tayenaka, Torrey. "Beginner's Guide to Social Media Marketing." *Entrepreneur Magazine*, Irvine, CA. https://www.entrepreneur.com/article/353848

Image Credits

Entrepreneur
kids

Contents
all about social media

WHAT IS *social media?*

Social media is the term used for the sharing of thoughts, information, and ideas on the internet through virtual communities. These virtual communities are also called **platforms**. There are different types of platforms for social media. There are:

- **Photo sharing sites like Instagram and Snapchat**
- **Video sharing sites like TikTok and YouTube**
- **Social sharing sites like Facebook**
- **Blogging sites like Twitter**

Many people use social media to connect with others for fun, but you can also use it for your business, to advertise events, and to buy and sell products.

Did You Know?

There are 3.81 billion people on social media according to Statista. That's more than 50 percent of the Earth's population!

important!

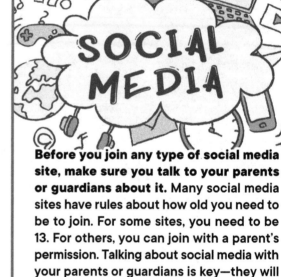

Before you join any type of social media site, make sure you talk to your parents or guardians about it. Many social media sites have rules about how old you need to be to join. For some sites, you need to be 13. For others, you can join with a parent's permission. Talking about social media with your parents or guardians is key—they will need to know which social media accounts you are using and what you are using them for. Read on for ways you can be a responsible and savvy social media user!

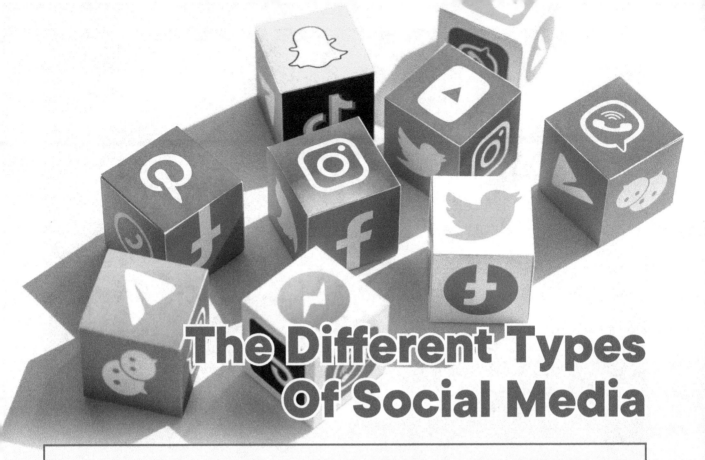

The Different Types Of Social Media

Social media is constantly changing. There are several different social media platforms that you can use today—some more popular than others. Doing a quick search on your phone or other device will give you lots of different social media apps. Often the ones you end up using are the ones that let you connect with your friends and family. You wouldn't want to download a social media app that no one else you know is using, because then you'd have no one else to connect with!

Most social media apps allow you to share photos and short videos, but each app has a unique audience. So, what's the difference? Let's take a look.

Photo Sharing Apps

Do you like to take pictures? Do you love to take selfies? Do you take a million pictures of your dog or cat? If you do, then you've probably already heard of these photo sharing apps. There are several different photo sharing social media sites, such as **Instagram** and **Snapchat**. These types of sites are for sharing photographs and short videos. Each app is special in its own way and can be fun for different reasons. They often come with filters so you can create all sorts of fun effects for your pictures, like giving your dog a rabbit's nose or having fire or rainbows coming out of your mouth. There are all kinds of creative things you can do with these types of apps.

Keep Reading! ⟶

Video Sharing Apps

If creating short videos is your thing, then chances are you've heard of **TikTok**. TikTok is one of the most popular video sharing apps out there. These types of apps are specifically for sharing short videos and most of these apps also come with filters. You can add music, dancing, graphics, and all sorts of special effects to your videos.

Social Sharing Apps

There is some overlap here between photo sharing apps and social sharing apps. Social sharing apps, like **Facebook**, also let you share pictures and short videos—so why don't they fall under photo sharing apps? Well, because you can *also* share ideas and information without showing a picture or video.

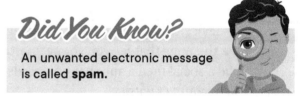

Did You Know?
An unwanted electronic message is called **spam.**

Blogging Apps

Blogging apps like **Twitter** are for mainly sharing information, thoughts, and ideas. You can also share pictures, but these types of sites were mostly created to share news and current events.

Now that you know what the different types of social media are, you can start to think about what kind of social media apps you may be interested in. Which one suits you best? What do you think you could use social media for? ⬤

SOCIAL MEDIA AND
communication

The way we communicate with others is a lot different than it used to be. Just 30 years ago, if you wanted to talk to your friend after school, you had to call them from a phone that was connected to a wall! Can you imagine that? If you were lucky, the phone would have a long cord so you could sit down and talk. Today, it is normal for people to have their own phones. And phones are used for so much more than just talking. What are the different ways you communicate? Let's look at some of the most common ones.

Keep Reading!

Video Chat

Using a video chat is another fun way to communicate with friends and family. If you're too far away to meet in-person, then having a face-to-face conversation with the help of a device is the next best thing.

Post on Social Media

Social media is just another form of communication. It's not just how people keep in touch! One of the big differences between social media and other forms of communication is that social media lets you communicate with many people all at the same time and from all over the world. If you own a business and you want to sell something, would you want to advertise on social media? Definitely! If you advertise on social media, you're going to be able to reach a lot of people and hopefully those people will buy your product so you can make lots of money.

Send a Text

Text messaging is good for short messages. If you want to let your mom or dad know that you're done with volleyball practice, then a text message is a great choice.

Send an Email

If you have a longer message to write, then an email is your best bet. Emailing is a good way to communicate with your teachers and family that are far away.

Did You Know?

A **network** is a group of things that are connected. Social media is considered a network. You may have heard an adult say that they are "networking." This means they are talking or emailing with someone they want to do business with.

why use SOCIAL MEDIA?

The obvious answer is to socialize with other people. Social media is a way to communicate with friends and family no matter how far away they are. If you live in California and you have cousins in New York, you can keep in touch with them through social media by sharing photos and videos even though you live 3000 miles apart. What are some other reasons, though, to use social media?

- **To advertise a product**
- **To promote a song**
- **To share an opinion**
- **To read about news and current events**

Think about your favorite product, such as a pair of shoes, a type of makeup, or a bike. Do you see your favorite product advertised on social media? If so, do you like the advertisement? Does it make you want to buy more of the product? People can make a lot of money advertising on social media, which is the reason so many companies use it to promote their businesses.

devices FOR SOCIAL MEDIA

When people think of social media, they automatically think of **smartphones.** Although smartphones are one type of device to use for social media, you can also use other devices too, such as **tablets**, **laptops**, and **desktop computers.**

Did You Know?

A **firewall** is a security feature that prevents unwanted online connections.

ALL ABOUT YOUR *digital* FOOTPRINT

Have you ever heard the term "digital footprint"? It sounds kind of mysterious, doesn't it? A **digital footprint** is a data trail of everything you have done online. Think of it like this: When a criminal commits a crime, police officers use the criminal's physical footprints to track them down. You can guess a lot about someone from their footprint, such as height and weight. Well, in a similar way, people leave traces of themselves virtually every time they use the internet.

Each time you go online to look up something, your computer remembers it. Each time you use social media to post or comment on someone else's post, you leave behind your digital footprint with likes or comments. Every single time you are online, you leave traces of what you did. This is important to remember because as you get older, everything you do online can be tracked. Even if you delete a post or a comment, the app you are using remembers it. This can impact whether a college admits you, whether you get hired for a job, or any number of things. So, remember: Always be kind to other people in your posts and comments.

After playing a game online or looking something up, have you noticed ads relating to what you were doing? The digital footprint you leave behind can even change the type of ads that you see. For example, if you look up new skateboards, you may notice that skateboard ads suddenly appear the next time you go online. So, remember, no matter what you do online, you are leaving a digital footprint behind.

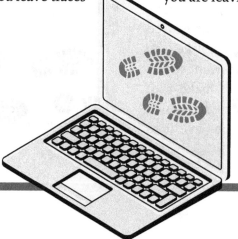

1 What do you think about using social media to communicate with other people? Do you think it is a good thing or a bad thing? Why?

2 Why do you think future employers might look up your social media account?

3 Do you think it's fair if you get in trouble because of something you've posted?

Did You Know?

Phishing is when you receive an email, call, or text from someone pretending to be someone they're not with the intention of getting personal information from you. For example, if you ordered something from Amazon and then a few weeks later you receive a text from someone pretending to be from Amazon wanting a payment, chances are someone is phishing for you to give them your information. Don't do it. Always tell an adult if you get a message that doesn't sound right.

Find the words that are hidden in the puzzle. Words may be forward, backward, diagonal, horizontal, or vertical.

```
L I A B B L O G G I N G
P P A D V E R T I S E A
T N I R P T O O F S I W
D I G I T A L B M D L P
V B A P Z L T A E B I L
T S O P S N R M O Z A A
U Z V H E T L E Y O M T
Z E A M P A M B G F E F
M R M H I G Z N Y W G O
E O O C G E C I V E D R
C N O Y L H I U Z S M M
E S C P L A U T R I V T
```

SOCIAL MEDIA   APP   DIGITAL   COMMENT
DEVICE   PLATFORM   FOOTPRINT   ADVERTISE
BLOGGING   VIRTUAL   SMARTPHONE
EMAIL   POST   SHARE

ANSWER KEY ON PAGE 53

Oh no! Jack lost his phone and his parents are very upset with him. Help Jack find his phone by going through the maze.

ANSWER KEY ON PAGE 53

creating
USERNAMES AND PASSWORDS

When creating your social media accounts (or any online accounts), the first thing you will need to do is create a username and password. Seems pretty simple, right? Well, not so fast. There are a few things you need to take into consideration first.

Usernames

If you're creating a social media account for the first time, you want your username to be something catchy, but you also don't want it to be something that you'll outgrow. For example, if you're 11 and just creating a social media account, you want your username to be something that your 13-year-old self will also like. Try to be as generic as possible so that your username won't embarrass you later on.

Passwords

Passwords are very important. No one should be able to guess your password and if they can, then it's not a good password. Make sure your password is long enough and includes a mix of letters, numbers, and special characters (like the & or % symbols). The longer your password, the harder it is for someone to guess. A good rule to use when creating a password is to make it at least eight characters long.

Some Password Don'ts

Never ever use any personal information in your password, such as your:

- name
- birthday
- email address
- home address
- phone number

Password Storage

Keep a copy of your usernames and passwords in a safe place and always make sure your parents know where they are. You don't want anyone to find them or guess them. Passwords are private information meant to keep your accounts safe.

Create a Password by Making Up a Sentence

An excellent way to come up with a strong password that's difficult to guess is to think of a sentence you can easily remember. For example, take a sentence like "My favorite animal is the koala bear." Now take the first letter of each word in the sentence, throw in some punctuation and replace some of those letters with numbers for variety. That sentence can be converted into a password like this:

My favorite animal is the koala bear = mFA1tkB!

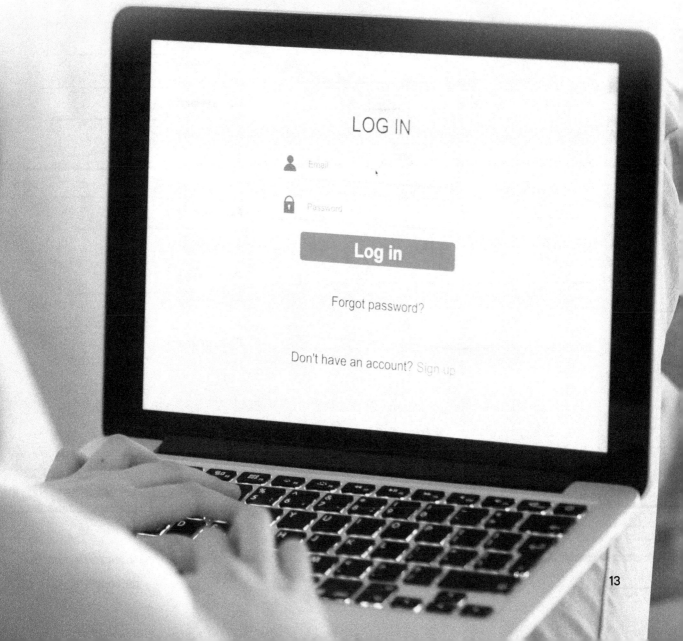

LOG IN

Email

Password

Log in

Forgot password?

Don't have an account? Sign up

Password Fun

Fill in the blanks to come up with passwords that are not only hard to guess, but easy for you to remember! Remember to replace at least one letter with a number and to add one type of punctuation to the password.

My favorite animal is the _____. **Password:**

My best friend loves the color _____. **Password:**

I was born in _____ and have _____ eyes. **Password:**

I love dressing up for _____ in _____. **Password:**

Now try making up your own sentences to use for passwords.

_____. **Password:**

_____. **Password:**

_____. **Password:**

Did You Know?

A man named **Fernando Corbato** invented the computer password. He worked at Massachusetts Institute for Technology (MIT) when he had to figure out a way for multiple people to be able to use a computer at the same time.

Entrepreneur kids

ALL ABOUT SOCIAL MEDIA

safety

Using social media comes with the responsibility to use it wisely. When you use social media safely, it can be a lot of fun. Here are some safety tips to keep in mind.

Privacy Settings

Ask your adults to check your privacy settings. Most social media apps will include only some safety requirements in the settings. For example, your social media accounts should be private—not public—accounts. This way anything you post will only be visible to your friends. Don't let people you don't know follow you on social media.

Friend Requests

Only accept requests from people you know. And, make sure they are actual people. It may sound silly, but sometimes tricky and unsafe strangers will try to friend you by pretending to be a favorite character. For example, if you are a big Harry Potter fan and someone sends you a friend request with the name Ron Weasley, you might think it's funny and accept the request. But, in real life (IRL), you have no idea who this supposed "Ron Weasley" really is. The safest thing to do is delete the request and tell your trusted adults.

Keep Reading! →

Beware of Fake Accounts

Have you heard of spam accounts? **Spam accounts** are fake profiles of people you know in real life that are often used for cyberbullying. If a friend of yours sends you another friend request, look at their profile before accepting their request to make sure it's really them. If it looks off or something seems not right, don't accept the request.

Location, Location, Location

When posting on social media, disable the location settings on your device. If you don't know how to do that, ask your trusted adults. Never share your location on social media. If you're at the mall and you post a picture, don't include which mall you're at and try not to show things in the background of your picture that give away your location. This helps keep you safe.

Offline Meeting Is a Big No

If you do meet someone new online either through social media or by playing an online video game, never agree to meet this person offline. Even if this person seems like someone you think you trust, the truth is you don't really know them. If someone does ask you to meet them somewhere, make sure you not only don't go, but that you tell your parents or another trusted adult.

Before you post something on social media, take a few minutes to think about what you're posting. Remember that words can sometimes be very hurtful. Post positive things!

Commenting

If your cousin posts a picture of her dog, let her know how cute Fido is! It's okay to comment on the posts from people you know. Always be kind with your comments. Have you ever heard the saying, "If you don't have anything nice to say, don't say anything at all?" Well, that's how you should approach social media. If you don't like someone else's post, just don't comment. Keep scrolling!

Sharing

It's okay to share pictures, but there are some things for you to consider first. If you love taking pictures and want to share pictures of the cute animals you saw during a hike you took, go for it. Sharing your love for photography with friends and family can be a lot of fun. Just be aware of what you're posting. Be aware that *all* of your friends and family who are your social media friends can see your pictures. Don't post pictures that you wouldn't be proud of taking.

H2 Sharing

Making short videos to post is easier than ever, but try to focus your videos on something you love to do. For example, if you are totally into drawing, make short videos featuring your artwork. Or try creating your own cooking show. Think of things that you will not only have fun doing in a video, but things that show off your talent or hobby.

17

Your Instagram Page

Make your own Instagram homepage. Draw your own profile picture. How many posts have you made? How many followers to you have? How many people are you following? In each box, draw or write your own posts!

www.instagram.com

Entrepreneur Kids

Posts   **Followers**   **Following**

SOCIAL MEDIA smarts

What Does It Mean to Go Viral?

When a video, image, or text goes **viral**, it means that it has been shared and seen by a lot of people. Usually, a post has to be shared by thousands of people in order to go viral. Not everyone agrees on how many people have to share something in order for it to be considered "viral," but usually something has to be shared by enough people in a short amount of time that nearly everyone you know has heard about it.

What Is Real and What Is Fake?

False or fake information is a big problem on social media. **Fake information** is something that gets shared online but isn't true. Sometimes it's hard to tell real information from what is false or fake. As technology has gotten more advanced, it has become easier and easier to manipulate pictures and news articles so they look real. It's important to remember that not everything you see or read online is true. So how do you know what's real and what's fake? Here are some questions to ask yourself if you see something that you're not sure about:

- **Where is the picture, video, or article coming from?** Is it from a professional news organization? Or is it from a source you've never heard of?

- **Is it giving someone's opinion or is it a fact?** If it is someone's opinion, beware of it. Everyone has their own opinion, but opinions are just someone's point of view.

- **Is someone trying to sell something?** If someone wants you to buy something, then chances are it's not actual news.

- **When in doubt, do your own research.** Don't automatically believe what you see or read online.

Keep Reading! ⟶

I've Heard You Can Buy Friends or Followers Online. Is That True?

Yes, this is true. Companies can buy followers to make them look like they have a lot of them. The problem is the followers they buy may not be interested in what they are selling. They may not even be active accounts. You can tell that someone has fake followers by looking at their comments. Do they make sense? If someone has 10,000 followers, but no one ever comments on their posts, chances are most of those followers are fake.

What Is Clickbait?

Clickbait is a post or link that is designed to get your attention. Whoever created the clickbait wants you to click on it. It could be a link or a picture that is designed to attract your attention so that you click on it. The headline for clickbait is something overly exaggerated and usually disappointing or not what it promised to be once you click on it.

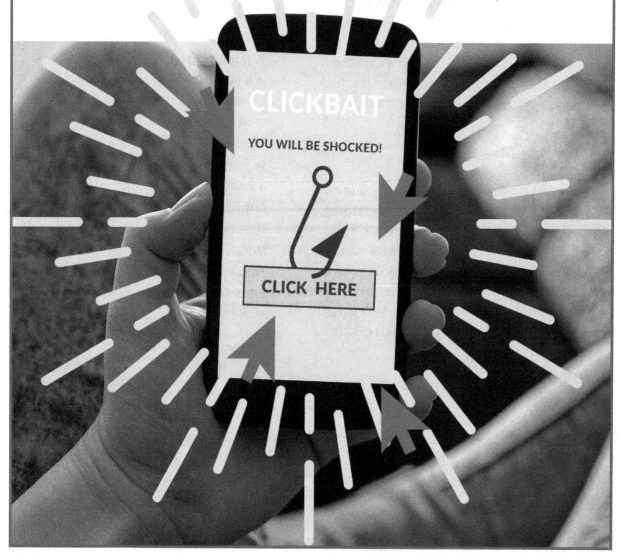

crossword

ACROSS

2. When you leave a ____ on someone's post, it should always be positive.

3. Always turn your location settings off when you ____ a picture.

6. A ____ footprint will stay with you for the rest of your life.

10. ____ is something designed to get your attention, but usually isn't what you think it is.

DOWN

1. A term for exchanging information or ideas.

4. Another term for posting a picture or an idea.

5. Another term for a smartphone.

7. Always check your ____ settings to make your social media accounts are secure.

8. ____ information is a term for something posted online that isn't real.

9. You need to have a good, strong ____ to prevent others from using your account.

ANSWER KEY ON PAGE 53

SOCIAL MEDIA AND *school*

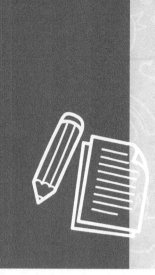

Most schools use some form of technology in classrooms like computers, laptops, or tablets. Some teachers also use social media to communicate with their students. It could be a blog that is used for class discussions or a private group on a platform like Facebook or Instagram that allows students to post pictures for a project. There are many ways that social media can be incorporated into classrooms. What are ways your school uses social media?

Have you ever been assigned a group project where you've had to exchange email, text, or instant messages with your classmates? Or have you needed help with an assignment and sent your classmates a message asking for help studying? All of these are ways that social media can be helpful in school.

AVOID online drama

Have you ever had friendship drama? Maybe now that you're in middle school, you and your best friend are not agreeing on the things you used to agree on. Or maybe you have a new student in your class and your best friend is suddenly talking to him and not to you. There are lots of different situations that can create friendship drama. Some drama is part of life. As people change and grow, so do their likes and dislikes. This is normal. Social media drama is a bit new. Chances are your parents didn't have to deal with social media drama when they were in elementary and junior high school. Why? Well, because social media didn't exist then!

Keep Reading! ⟶

Social media drama can start with just a misunderstanding. The problem is usually something called context. **Context** is extra information about an event that helps you understand it better. For example, let's say, Marissa posts a picture of her new haircut and Kelly sees the picture and comments, "Wow. It's short!" Then Marissa sees Kelly's comment and thinks Kelly hates her hair and doesn't want to go to school because she thinks everyone is going to make fun of her new short hair.

What if Kelly didn't mean her comment in a bad way? What if she really liked it, but it didn't seem that way when she posted her words? She left out important context that would have helped Marissa understand her comments better. When you write something, it can be hard for other people to understand the context or meaning behind what you wrote. They don't know if you're smiling or making a joke. They can't see your face or your body language. This can lead to misunderstandings and online drama.

Hiding Behind a Screen

Sometimes people say things online they would never say in person. Why do you think this is? Usually, it's because when you post something online, you don't have to see the other person face-to-face. No one is looking back at you. You might feel braver commenting online because other people don't know you. This can create a lot of online drama. Just because people can't see you doesn't mean you're not responsible for what you say.

Did You Know?

The most common type of online bullying come from mean comments and the spreading of untrue rumors.

After you write a post and before you hit send, reread it. Does it make sense? Did you leave out a word that changes the meaning of what you wanted to say? Remember that social media is about interacting with other people online. What you say can hurt someone's feelings even if that wasn't your intention. You can delete things, but sometimes people will have seen what you posted before you delete it. Remember: Don't share news that isn't yours to share. If it involves another person, let them share the news.

Before you make a post, ask yourself these questions:

- **Is your post kind?**
- **Are you making a comment that someone may not understand?**
- **Would you be okay with a college admissions officer seeing this post?**
- **Would your future employer be okay with seeing this post?**
- **Is the post embarrassing to someone else?**

SOCIAL MEDIA *beware*

There are downsides to social media. Have you heard of online trolls? **Online tolls** are people who purposely want to start an argument with someone else. They want to make you get upset. Online trolls often comment on someone's post not only to be mean, but to start a fight between other people. They love creating online drama. Just like a dangerous animal at the zoo, you should not give them what they want. Don't feed the trolls!

Keep Reading! ⟶

All About Online Bullying

At some point, friends are going to disagree, but there is a big difference between disagreements and bullying. Cyberbullies are similar to online trolls and, in fact, sometimes these are the same people. A **cyberbully** is just like an in-person bully, but they do all of their bullying online.

Cyberbullying happens online. It is not something teachers or parents are likely to see. If adults don't know it's happening, they can't help stop it. It's very important to tell an adult if you think you or someone you know is being cyberbullied. In some states, cyberbullying is even against the law.

Cyberbullies want to embarrass you. They want to hurt or intimidate you. You may feel badly about yourself because of it and not know what to do. Aside from telling an adult, there are some things you can do:

- **Take a break from social media.** Turn your devices off and ignore them for a few days.

- **Don't engage with someone who makes mean comments online.** Just ignore them, block them, or unfriend them from your accounts.

- **Remember that if someone is cyberbullying you, it is not your fault.** The person doing the bullying is the one with the problem. By telling an adult, you are helping them get help and preventing them from cyberbullying other people. K

THINKING ABOUT
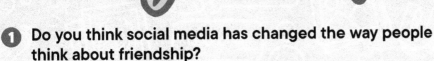
online friendships

1 Do you think social media has changed the way people think about friendship?

2 Why do people want to "collect" online friends or followers?

3 Do you think people who have more social media followers have more "real" friends than you do? Why or why not?

MEET A SOCIAL MEDIA ENTREPRENEUR: Laurence Moss

When Laurence Moss was 12, he decided to try his hand at becoming a YouTuber. It was a quick and hard lesson in cyberbullying. As he recalls, "Videos of me talking to a camera seemed to be something that people liked to make fun of." So, he switched gears. At 13, he tried Instagram, experimenting with accounts themed around everything from memes to cars, with less of an emphasis on his own face and personality. By the end of 2018, he had well over a quarter-million followers.

The following year, having only just turned 14, Moss launched his own marketing agency, Greedy Growth, from his home in Kent, UK. In the company's own words, it exists to "turn your Instagram page into a marketing asset." His clients include soccer star Joel Mumbongo and health-food brand Ossa Organic. In 2020, the company earned five figures!

What is it like to run a company from your home with a remote team while attending school?

Laurence Moss: There's staff based in lots of different countries. I've got people in different positions throughout the company to do different tasks. One of the reasons why I've been able to do so much while being in school and being young is because I've been able to recognize the things that I need to delegate so that I can put the time I have in the right places.

Is this a balancing act you think most students could pull off or are you just uniquely cut out for it?

LM: I never went into it thinking of myself as an entrepreneur. It grew out of a hobby for me, sort of wanting to build communities on Instagram. I had about a year when I wasn't making money from it. Not everybody can balance it. It really just depends on the person.

How did you convince people who were weren't sure about signing on with your company because of your youth?

LM: When I launched my company, I was

> ## "I never went into it thinking of myself as an entrepreneur. It grew out of a hobby for me, sort of wanting to build communities on Instagram."

14, and I was getting on calls with business owners. As, long as I had the confidence of knowing my craft, which was Instagram marketing, then they were confident to trust me with their marketing money. But there are always going to be the business owners who try to haggle you down and try to take advantage of your age. It's just about having the understanding that I'm not going to change the price that I offer my services for if they think they can get that because of my age.

Did anyone help you get to where you are today? Was it family? Did you have entrepreneurs you admired?

LM: I look up to people, but I wouldn't say I had someone holding my hand. And I think that part of the reason I got to the point where I am now is because I was a self-starter. Nobody held my hand or told me to do any of this. If I didn't have that drive to try and find things out for myself and be curious, I don't think it would have come about in the first place.

It also sounds like you're still on the fence about whether to continue juggling studies and your company down the line?
LM: I still might want to go to college. It's not something that I've decided yet. There is a likelihood of me deciding when the time comes around that I don't want to go to college, and that I want to pursue the business full-time.

Did You Know?

An **entrepreneur** is someone who starts their own business.

Keep Reading! ⟶

> "Nobody held my hand or told me to do any of this. If I didn't have that drive to try and find things out for myself and be curious, I don't think it would have come about in the first place."

Instagram and social media marketing are everywhere. Are you keeping an eye out for the next best thing?

LM: I think there's always going to be audiences that hang out on social media platforms. As long as you're staying ahead in terms of the trends happening on those social media platforms, there's always a way to reach that audience. So, for example, when TikTok was released, it drew some attention away from Instagram, but they made Reels, which tried to grab a little bit of that back. I see Instagram being fairly long term, but obviously you never really know what's going to come around and be the next Instagram.

Did You Know?

A **consumer** is someone who purchases goods or services for their own personal use. Everyone is a consumer of something, from toothpaste to clothes to the type of food we eat.

Is there a goal for you as the company becomes more profitable?

LM: What makes me most happy is not necessarily the money side of things, but my idea growing. Early this year, we started working with professional British footballers, and it's really interesting to me how I can take this idea and turn it into something that's actually real and then make an impact.

What would you say now to the people who used to cyberbully you?

LM: It's all about empathy and understanding. I don't hate anybody for any decisions or actions that they make. Many of the people who did those sorts of things back then, I'm now quite good friends with. I think the whole reason why I persevered is because I've learned to sort of stay in my own lane. Other people's decisions or other people's thoughts don't really make a difference to me. I've got the support of close friends and family and what they say to me does have an impact. ⊗

unplug
ONCE IN A WHILE

Technology is a big part of our lives. From the moment you wake up in the morning and pick up your phone to end the alarm, to the time you spend checking social media, technology is constantly there. If you've been feeling less productive than usual, it may be that your devices are taking up too much of your time. Although technology has improved many things, it can also have a downside if you're relying on it too much. Research has shown that you can be addicted to your devices, and with that addiction comes a decline in productivity, creativity, and joy. It might be time to unplug!

Taking a break from your devices can help you reset your brain so that you're not relying too much on your devices to plan your life, help you with your homework, or keep you entertained. Here are a few things you can do when you need to take a digital break.

Keep Reading! ⟶

Did You Know?

A **digital detox** is to stop using electronic devices, such as phones, computers, and tablets for a period of time.

Power It Down

Put down your phone and close your laptop. Take a hike, go for a swim, play a board game, read a book, and make it a habit. When you wait in line at a store, let yourself be bored, and see what comes up instead of scrolling on your phone. What do you think about? Give yourself times for being on-screen and times for turning your devices off for a while.

Turn Off Notifications

Turn off all notifications while you do your homework. Put your phone on night or airplane mode, turn off notifications, and make sure your chats are on away mode. If you need to check your devices, do so on scheduled breaks after a significant amount of homework time—say, 45 minutes to an hour.

Set a Time to Check Social Media

Take some time in the morning to just be. Wake up slowly, drink some water, and don't check your social media. If you have a tendency to read on your phone in bed, keep your phone across the room so you can't check it first thing in the morning. Buy an analog clock with an alarm so your phone isn't a necessity. Set a time later in the day to check social media, messages, and emails and stick to a time limit.

With a little bit of effort, you can change the amount of time you spend on technology and you may be surprised on how much your productivity improves without even noticing that it's happening. Remember—keep a balance between IRL relationships and technology!

Try A 7-Day Digital Challenge

DAY	GOAL
1	Put your phone on the other side of your room at night (so you can't reach it).
2	After school, don't look at your phone until you're done with homework.
3	Delete any apps that you no longer use.
4	Only look at one social media account for no more than one hour.
5	Only look at one social media account for no more than half an hour.
6	No social media all day.
7	**Don't use your phone all day!**

Did you meet the challenge? If not, why? If so, good job! Write how you felt each day of the challenge.

1

2

3

4

5

6

7

email:
THE ORIGINAL SOCIAL MEDIA

There is a lot of debate about how social media really got started. Some people say the credit goes to a platform called Six Degrees in 1997. This website allowed users to create a profile, make friends, and share messages. Other people say it was actually started years before that with email.

Email is one of the most basic methods of technology that you need to know how to use. Email is like letter writing only it's done on the computer and is more formal than texting. As you get older, it is how you will communicate with your teachers.

Do you know what CC/BCC means in an email? **CC** means carbon copy and **2** means blind carbon copy. For example, if you are emailing your teacher and you want your parents to know what you wrote, you can include their email address on the CC line—it just means that they'll get a copy of the email you sent so they'll know what's going on.

But if you are emailing your teacher and you want your parents to know, but you don't want your teacher to know you're copying your parents on the email, you can add their email

address to the BCC line. Then they'll get a copy of the email, but your teacher won't know. Phew—that's kind of complicated! You probably won't need to use the BCC feature of email until your older and using email for work.

Sample Email

TO: afernandez@sample.com   CC: momanddad@sample.com

SUBJECT: School Election   BCC:

Hi Mrs. Fernandez,
I am excited to be running for student council! Can you let me know what the rules are for campaigning? Am I allowed to make posters? Or hand buttons out? Please let me know what the rules are when you get a chance.

Thank you for your time,
Kate M.

SEND   A ✏ 🖼 ☺ 🔗 🗑 | ☰

Now, you try writing an email to a teacher. It can be about anything you'd like!

TO: yourteacher@sample.com   CC:

SUBJECT: BCC:

SEND   A ✏ 🖼 ☺ 🔗 🗑 | ☰

SOCIAL MEDIA smarts

What Is Digital Literacy?

Digital literacy mean knowing how to use computers and the internet. Being able to go online and use social media is part of it, but you also need to know the downsides of being online. Do you think you are digitally literate? Do you think your parents or grandparents are?

What Is Malware?

Malware is short for malicious software. It takes over a computer when you click on a bad link or open an email attachment from someone you don't know. There are different names for malware, such as viruses, worms, adware, spyware, and Trojan horses. They all hurt your computer. Some steal passwords, others delete files, and some can stop your computer from working at all. So how do you prevent this from happening? Well, the

best way is to make sure you have security software installed on your devices. Don't click on ads that pop up when you're online. Do not open attachments from people you don't know. Always show a parent if you're not sure.

What Are Cookies?

Who doesn't like cookies? Computer cookies are very different from the warm, yummy treats you may be used to. These kinds of **cookies** are actually small pieces of data, like a username and password, that are used to identify your computer or device while you're online. Cookies are used to track your online viewing habits and then that information is sold to companies that then market and advertise to you. For example, let's say you really want a new backpack and you search

online for backpacks. The websites that you visit will often use cookies to keep track of you. And then the next time you go online, chances are you'll see advertisements for different backpacks.

What Is a Pop-Up Ad and How Can I Get Rid of It?

Pop-up ads can be very annoying. They are exactly how they sound. Pop-up ads are advisements that pop up when you are on a website. You can prevent pop-up ads by changing the security settings on your device. The way to do this is slightly different on different devices so ask a parent how to turn pop-ups off on your devices. And, remember, many pop-ups contain malware so don't click on them even if you're tempted.

USING SOCIAL MEDIA TO MAKE *money*

You can make money with social media. Companies use social media to advertise their products and sometimes people become social media influencers. There are other ways to make money on social media, though. If you are really good at making things, like handmade crafts or knitting, you can post them on social media and see if anyone wants to buy one. If you decide you want to tutor some local kids in a particular subject, you can promote your tutoring business on social media.

What Is a Social Media Influencer?

A **social media influencer** is a person who has a large following on their account, and they "influence" those followers to buy things. Often, they are known to be "experts" on a certain topic. You don't have to be a celebrity to be a social media influencer. It can be anyone who has a large audience. Social media influencers make posts about new products or ideas that influence other people to buy them. Sometimes a company will pay a social media influencer to post positive things about their product. Being a social media influencer may sound like a great job, but it's not easy and it takes a lot of work to build up followers.

advertising & marketing
ON SOCIAL MEDIA

Advertising and marketing are all over social media. Advertisements can be sneaky; you may not even realize that what you're looking at is an advisement. Whenever you see something online that says "Sponsored," that means it's really an advertisement. Let's say you have your own money-making idea like making tie-dyed T-shirts and you want to sell them to your friends, family, and neighbors. What are ways that you can market and advertise your business on social media?

Know Your Product and Your Customers

First, you will need to make posts that appeal to your customers. When you are first starting out, you know who you want to sell to—friends, family, neighbors—so what are the kinds of posts that will get their attention? Also, think about things they won't like and stay away from those kinds of posts.

Understand the Platform

Think about which platform you'll be using to advertise on. Are you using Instagram? TikTok? No matter which one you choose (you can also choose more than one), make sure you know how to use it. Are you posting pictures? Videos? Just words? Make sure your posts are well-written, not too long, and interesting. If you post a picture of your T-shirts and someone makes a comment that they're interested in buying one, make sure you respond to their comment. Ⓚ

SOCIAL MEDIA *careers*

Do you think having a career in social media is for you? Many people who work in social media have college degrees in communications, marketing, or advertising. Here are some different job titles that people who work in social media have:

- **Social media influencer**
- **Social media manager**
- **Social media consultant**
- **Digital media supervisor**
- **Brand manager**
- **Social media strategist**
- **Social media analyst**
- **Online community manager**
- **Engagement coordinator**

If you're serious about having a career in social media, research some of the job titles above so you can see what the job descriptions are and what the job requirements are. Some of these jobs average $94,000 a year! It's never too early to start thinking about your future!

DREAMING ABOUT WORKING IN
social media

If you could have a career in social media, which career would you pick?
Would you want to be an influencer? Why or why not?

SOCIAL MEDIA
word search

Find the words that are hidden in the puzzle. Words may be forward, backward, horizontal, or vertical.

```
Z Y N U D P U P O P L M
S Y O H A B I V I R U S
P L I N F L U E N C E R
R L T M D N G U K I Q Z
O U A T S D N N E F F V
D B C X E N I P R B O E
U R I E C V T L A K L I
C E F T A O E U W W L K
T B I N R V K G L O O O
H Y T O E F R J A F W O
E C O C E V A Y M N E C
I K N K R M M R U Z R X
```

MONEY
MARKETING
MALWARE
CONTEXT

UNPLUG
VIRUS
CYBERBULLY
PRODUCT

COOKIE
NOTIFICATION
POP UP
FOLLOWER

CAREER
INFLUENCER

ANSWER KEY ON PAGE 54

Create A Good Post

Let's practice writing social media posts! In the box at the top, write your name, or the name of your business on social media.

1 Write a post sharing information about something.

2 Write a post sharing an idea.

3 Write a post promoting your business.

4 Write a post asking a question about what your customers like.

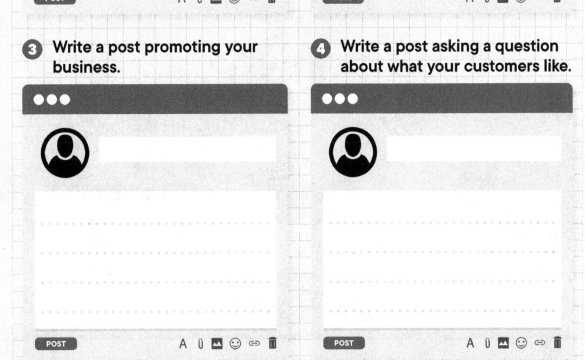

MEET THE *kid influencers*

Having fun and posting with your friends is a great way to stay connected when you can't be together in person. You can also use social media to share your hobbies, interests, or business idea with a bigger audience. Many kid entrepreneurs are also social media influencers. An influencer is someone who shares information about products and services on social media.

Let's meet some of the biggest kid influencers (and their families!) on YouTube and Instagram. Be ready to be amazed at all they share. And shout out to the parents who make it all possible, because we're guessing they are the ones doing a lot of the filming, art directing and uploading!

Action Movie Kids

 bit.ly/3yeLdGR

1.17 million subscribers

James and his little sister Sophia are the children of Daniel Hashimoto, who works as a special effects artist on popular films such as *Kung Fu Panda 2* and *How to Train Your Dragon*. Hashimoto puts his expertise to work transforming his kids' imaginary play into eye-catching videos.

Ryan's World

bit.ly/3rxavxd

30.1 million subscribers

Ryan's unboxing and toy review videos have reportedly earned him and his family a whopping $11 million a year, with a majority of the toys featured on the channel donated to charity. His channel also features skits, music, science experiments, and DIY challenges.

Hailey's Magical Playhouse

bit.ly/3kMXRsD

2.2 million subscribers

Hailey reviews and unboxes toys, most of which are given to charity, plays dress up, cooks in the kitchen (with supervision) and goes on family vacations, all of which can be seen on the channel, which launched in 2015.

WHAT IS *bit.ly?*

Each entry in this list includes a bit.ly web site address. **Bit.ly** is a way to take a long, complicated address, like to a channel on YouTube (▶), or to an Instagram profile (◻), and make it easier to type in to a web browser. If you have any problems, ask an adult for help!

Naiah and Ellie: The Cray Crays

bit.ly/3x2HNVU

1.9 million subscribers

Sister duo Naiah and Ellie began their YouTube journey with *Naiah and Ellie's Toy Show*. Viewers watched the sisters do skits, play with and unbox toys, and take trips to their local playgrounds. Now, the whole family is in on the fun with *Naiah and Ellie: The Cray Crays*. The family sitcom channel follows the adventures of the whole family, including their grandma, Sweetmomma.

Keep Reading! ⟶

Scout the City

@scoutthecity or bit.ly/3y2HgVw
351,000 followers

London Scout, little sibling Rio, and their mom pose in stylish looks around New York City. The family's fashion sense can be found mostly on Instagram, but they have an active YouTube channel as well.

Coco

@coco_pinkprincess or
bit.ly/3BAhzO7
619,000 followers

You wish you had as much attitude as this young fashion blogger from Tokyo. Coco is from Harajuku, Tokyo, and loves sharing her fashion sense on Instagram. She uses color and scenery to showcase her style.

Ministylehacker

@ministylehacker or bit.ly/3iz98tC
261,000 followers

California kids Ryker, Grey, and Wyatt's high fashion flare is captured by mom Collette Wixom in Los Angeles. They are active on Instagram, sharing their adventures in California.

Txunamy

@txunamy or bit.ly/3BKOAZY
4.2 million followers
bit.ly/36Wkcf3
3.4 million subscribers

This young fashionista has looks that even grown-ups would consider imitating. You can catch her styles on Instagram and fun videos on YouTube where she shares "day in the life" tidbits as well as DIY content.

READY TO START YOUR OWN
youtube channel?

If you like making and sharing videos, you can start your own YouTube channel. Here are some tips to get started:

❶ Ask Your Parents For Help
Remember: social media (especially YouTube) can be seen by the world. Ask your parents for permission before setting up your channel. They can help you make sure it has privacy controls in place to keep you safe.

❷ Have A Unique Idea
Your channel should be focused on a theme. What do you love to talk about or do? Maybe you want to review toys, share gaming tips, or do science experiments. Find something that you love, and get ready to share it.

❸ Think of a Fun Name
Your channel name should tell viewers something about the topic of your channel. For example, if you review the latest video games, you could call it *Game Reviews You Can Use*.

❹ Share Your Knowledge
Viewers want to learn something, so be sure to show them how to do something, explain an idea, or review a product like a game or toy.

❺ Tell A Good Story
No matter what you choose to record on video, be sure you have a good story to share. If you are reviewing a toy, you could talk about how you play with it. If you are showing how to do a science project, you could share some science facts.

❻ Keep It Visual
Viewers don't just want to watch you talk; they want to see you *do* something. Position your camera so they can see all the action as you unbox, cook, do an experiment, or give a tour of a city.

Vivian is new to social media. Help her learn how it all works!

Clue	Scramble	Answer

1 Vivian sees something on a page that she thinks is neat. **What should she do?**

EKLI

☐☐☐☐

2 Vivian posted a picture of herself and a friend. Now she wants her friend to know about it. **What should she do?**

GTA

☐☐☐

3 Vivian sees something on her feed that she wants others to see too. **What should she do?**

ASREH

☐☐☐☐☐ .

4 Vivian wants to leave a message for someone on their post. **What should she do?**

MEOMCNT

☐☐☐☐☐☐☐

5 Vivian took a picture of her dog and wants to put it on her page. **What should she do?**

OSPT

☐☐☐☐

ANSWER KEY ON PAGE 54

SOCIAL MEDIA
smarts

How Do I Get People to Notice Me on Social Media?

If you want to build up your followers on social media, try posting inspirational quotes. People will often like the quotes and then share them with other people. Another way is to be funny. Post silly pictures of your dog or cat. Everyone likes to be entertained. Remember, though, that social media is another way of communicating with people. If you are a kind and thoughtful person, be kind and thoughtful on social media, too. It doesn't matter how many people follow you on social media or how many online "friends" you have. It's your real friends that matter.

What Is a Micro-Influencer and a Mega-influencer?

A **micro-influencer** is a person who is an influencer with less than 10,000 followers on social media. A **mega-influencer** is a person who is an influencer with hundreds of thousands or even millions of followers. Micro-influencers tend to be very knowledgeable in whatever their field is and people tend to trust their opinion more than they do a mega-influencer. Because mega-influencers have more followers, they can sometimes seem too famous and harder to relate to.

Keep Reading! ⟶

What Does Feed Mean?

A social media **feed** is the content that you see from other users. Your feed is where you see other people's posts.

What Is a Social Media Podcast?

A **podcast** is like a radio show but can be played anytime or anywhere, usually as part of a series. There is a lot of debate about whether podcasts are part of social media. Some people think you use social media to advertise a podcast and others think some podcasts can be used on social media. Regardless, a podcast is a way to distribute information through audio.

What Is a Hashtag?

A **hashtag (#)** is way of connecting your posts on social media to other posts on the same subject. For example, let's say you love cats and decide to post a picture of your cat on Instagram and use *#catsofinstagram* on your post. What that means is that anyone who goes to #catsofinstagram, will see your cat's picture (along with all the other cats who've been tagged on #catsofinstagram).

Solve this puzzle to reveal a fact about social media.

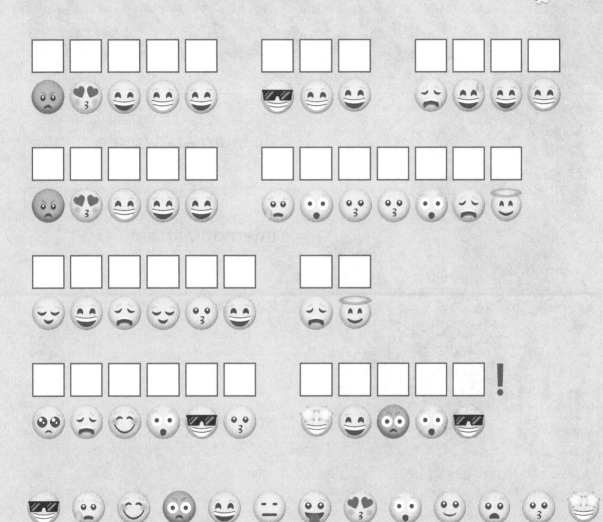

ANSWER KEY ON PAGE 54

SOCIAL MEDIA
resources

Be Internet Awsome
- beinternetawesome.
  withgoogle.com/en_us

Internet Matters
- internetmatters.org

Safe Search Kids
- safesearchkids.com/a-teens-
  guide-to-social-media-safety/
  #.YIDnOS1h3qO

StopBullying.gov
- stopbullying.gov/resources/
  get-help-now

puzzle solutions

Word Search page 10

```
L I A B B L O G G I N G
P P A D V E R T I S E A
T N I R P T O O F S I W
D I G I T A L B M D L P
V B A P Z L T A E B I L
T S O P S N R M O Z A A
U Z V H E T L E Y O M T
Z E A M P A M B G F E F
M R M H I G Z N Y W G O
E O O C G E C I V E D R
C N O Y L H I U Z S M M
E S C P L A U T R I V T
```

Crossword page 21

```
                    ¹C
                     O
              ²C O M M E N T
                     M
                     U        ³P O S T⁴
              ⁵D      N              H
               E      I        ⁶D I G I T A L
               V   ⁷P  ⁸F       C          R
               I    R   A    ⁹P  A          E
             ¹⁰C L I C K B A I T  S
               E    V   E    S
                    A        S
                    C        W
                    Y        O
                             R
                             D
```

Maze page 11

puzzle solutions

Word Search page 42

```
Z Y N U D P U P O P L M
S Y O H A B I V I R U S
P L I N F L U E N C E R
R L T M D N G U K I Q Z
O U A T S D N N E F F V
D B C X E N I P R Y O E
U R I E C V T L A E L I
C E F T A O E U W N L K
T B I N R V K G L O O O
H Y T O E F R J A M W O
E C O C E V A Y M N E C
I K N K R M M R U Z R X
```

Unscramble page 48

1 LIKE
2 TAG
3 SHARE
4 COMMENT
5 POST

Crack The Code page 51

THERE ARE OVER

THREE BILLION

PEOPLE ON

SOCIAL MEDIA!

CPSIA information can be obtained
at www.ICGtesting.com
Printed in the USA
JSHW040727310821
18292JS00002B/5